See the Light

and walk therein

"I'm black and I'm beautiful."

— King Solomon (Song of Solomon 1:5, KJV)

"My skin is black." — Job

(Job 30:30, KJV)

ISBN 978-1-7753947-4-7

Version 12.11.119.11. Updated May 23, 2025

Black History

New Dark Age

by Jason Drysdale

CONTENT

About the Author

Jason Drysdale is an inspirational wordsmith, covering the topics of history, health and wealth. His hobbies include yachting and flying. He is also a connoisseur of the finer things in life.

Never be limited by other people's limited imaginations. — Dr. Mae Jemison

Naked Truth

— The naked truth vs. the well-dressed lie —

Put on your diving suit for a moment - we're going to dive deep in search of the precious treasure that we call knowledge. Now, can you dive deep? If not, you can turn to another page. **However, if you have the guts to keep reading, then more power to you - you're a brave one indeed. Fortune favors the brave! So, without any further ado, let's dive in.**

Truth and Lie went swimming one day. Both took off their clothes and entered the water. While swimming, Naked Lie jumped out and stole Naked Truth's clothing.

Since that day, Naked Truth has been trying to catch up with the well-dressed Lie, who is masquerading in Truth's clothing.

There are multitudes of lies out there dressed up as Truth. One example is Beethoven being a white man (a well-dressed lie). **The fact is that Beethoven was black.**

Another lie is the image of Jesus with blond hair and blue eyes.

I'll admit that it shouldn't matter what color skin Jesus or Beethoven had, but for the sake of Truth, we need to catch and expose this well-dressed Lie.

There are countless inventions by individuals of African descent, yet only a handful of black inventors have received recognition. Because slave masters held slaves as property, the intellectual property of the slaves was claimed by the masters. They would take the inventions without giving proper credit to the enslaved individuals.

You may say that this sounds like bull, but consider this: The slaves were the ones doing the work, which leads to the fact that **adversity is the mother of creativity, and necessity is the mother of invention.**

Furthermore, truth is often stranger than fiction. We're so accustomed to seeing and hearing well-dressed lies that when the naked truth finally appears - it's hard for us to believe it.

And by the way, yes! The Naked Truth is catching up to the well-dressed Lie. So, let's get together and kick ass.

Shocking Facts

The original Jews are all black people. PROOF: The oldest Jews in Isreal today are all black folks - they live in the remote and mountainous parts of Isreal, and they've been there for thousands of years and a lot longer than the Caucasian Jews who recently migrated from Europe.

The greatest author in the history of France was a black man (Alexandre Dumas). He wrote The Three Musketeers, The Count of Monte Cristo, and many more. He remains the most widely-read novelist in the entire history of France.

The greatest poet in the history of Russia was a black man (Alexander Pushkin). PROOF: His great-grandfather was a black man from Africa.

Two black female students solved a math problem that Caucasians believed was impossible to solve for more than 2,000 years (Pythagoras theorem). Their remarkable achievement highlights black excellence and position them as true heroes within the black community (Calcea Johnson and Ne'Kiya Jackson).

All people originated from the black man. PROOF: Gregor Mendel (modern genetics) has proven that dark skin is dominant and light skin is recessive - you can inherit the recessive from the dominant - but you cannot inherit the dominant from the recessive.

The greatest composer of all time was a black man (Beethoven). PROOF: Fredrick Hertz (a white German anthropologist) studied Beethoven and concluded that he was black. Also, an acquaintance of Beethoven described him to be "a short and stocky black man."

The greatest agricultural scientist in the history of the United States was a black man (George Washington Carver). He created hundreds of inventions, including peanut butter.

The black man built the pyramids in Egypt. PROOF: The hieroglyphics on the walls inside the pyramids show that they were black. Furthermore, the most famous Egyptian pharaoh has the face of a pure black man with thick lips - a unique attribute of blacks (King Tutankhamun).

Jesus and Mary were blacks of African descent. PROOF: In the description of Jesus (Revelations 1:14-15), he had hair like wool and a dark complexion like burnt brass. In addition, Mary is portrayed as a black woman in many of the oldest churches in Europe.

In gymnastics, a black woman is the greatest gymnast in the history of America and the entire world - A shocking accomplishment, considering that blacks are only 13% of the population in America (Simone Biles).

Black people are blessed. They are the richest people on the planet (spiritually, physically, mentally and emotionally).

Black people are exceedingly beautiful. Yes, but some people eat pork, white flour, white sugar, white rice, and lots of fried food and gravy, which dulls their appearance and dims the light they carry. Nevertheless, every now and then, you'll see a black person who eats right and lives right - then you'll understand what I'm saying. They're the most beautiful and shapely people I've ever seen. The females have the shape of a Coco-Cola bottle, while the males have great physiques.

If everything was perfect, you would never learn and you would never grow. — Beyonce Knowles (the most-awarded female singer in the history of America).

Black Heroes

Marcus Garvey was the legendary black leader who fought for the freedom and dignity of his people. He created the U.N.I.A. in 1914 and inspired millions to fight for justice.

"Emancipate yourselves from mental slavery, none but ourselves can free our minds." - Marcus Garvey

Elijah Muhammad was a brilliant king-maker and a champion for freedom, justice, and equality. This divinely gifted leader has taught and empowered great men like Malcolm X, Muhammad Ali, Louis Farrakhan, and many more. Why is he head and shoulder above other great leaders? Only the very best leaders can take ordinary men and turn them into great heroes.

"I am not trying to get you to fight. That is not even necessary; our unity will win the battle! Not one of us will have to raise a sword. Not one gun would we need to fire. The great cannon that will be fired is our unity. Our unity is the best." - Elijah Muhammad

Harriet Tubman was the renowned heroine who freed many slaves. Born into slavery, Tubman escaped and made missions to rescue her fellow slaves using the underground railroad.

"I freed a thousand slaves, I could have freed a thousand more if only they knew they were slaves." - Harriet Tubman

Bessie Coleman was the first black female pilot in the United States and the first licensed black pilot in the world. She received aviation instruction in France - because she could not receive training in the United States (because of her skin color). She was eventually inducted into the National Aviation Hall Of Fame - A superb accomplishment of overcoming great odds and racial discrimination.

"The air is the only place free from prejudices". "I decided blacks should not have to experience the difficulties I had faced, so I decided to open a flying school and teach other black women to fly." - Bessie Coleman

Martin Luther King Jr. - Activist and leader of the Civil Rights Movement. King suffered and struggled for the cause of justice for the oppressed. He was the youngest person to win the Nobel Peace Prize in 1964.

"Whatever your life's work is, do it well. A man should do his job so well that the living, the dead, and the unborn could do it no better." - Martin Luther King Jr.

Inventions

— Inventions by the original man —

Potato Chips (George Speck/Crum). **Ice Cream** (Augustus Jackson). **Coffee** (Africans). **Traffic Light** (Garrett A. Morgan). **Civilization** (Africans). Plus many more... **NOTE:** There are thousands of black inventions, but in order to keep this book concise and interesting - I've listed just a few.

Nature's Definitions

— The correct definition of words —

Black: natural, rich, and healthy. Nature loves black, and nature gives us black in abundance - black grapes, black olives, black plums, blackberries, black beans, black rice, and many more. Also, the #1 spice in the world is black pepper, and the #1 beverage is black (coffee).

White: abnormal, processed, and artificial. Nature tends to avoid white (I have never seen a white fruit), and white is the only color or shade that cannot occur naturally by mixing other colors. **White also means negative space - we learn this as graphic designers and painters in school.**

NOTE: The definitions of black and white in Caucasian dictionaries are well-dressed lies. People subconsciously know that the blacker the berry, the sweeter the juice, and they know that they shouldn't consume white sugar or inhale white powder (both are extremely dangerous and addictive).

"To get lost is to learn the way." - Africa Proverb

Inner Views

Interview with the black history promoter: King Majesty

Before I start asking questions, thank you for agreeing to this interview. I'm delighted.

King Majesty is such a heroic name. Is this your real name? My nickname is Jason, but my real name is King Majesty. I was born in Kingston, Jamaica, and so the name was crafted - by using the first four letters of Kingston (King), and the first three letters of Jamaica (Jam). Then, by turning the Jam around, you get Maj - the short form for Majesty.

Interesting... What do you do for a living? I'm a wordsmith and a painter. I paint the hearts of men with the truth - by giving knowledge, wisdom, and understanding.

I like your work ethic. I have seen you in snowstorms and thunderstorms working. Why? Because I'm the foremost authority in the promotion of black history in Canada.

Define black. What's so special about black? Black is the essence of all things. All things originate from blackness, and according to historical scripture - man was created from black mud (Holy Quran, Surah 15, verses 26-29), and millions of pilgrims rally around a black stone every year in Mecca.

I also like your design. The front cover feels soft as velvet, and the back cover is as smooth as a baby's bottom. It is such a good design; I would not be surprised if you told me that people drool when they see it. But anyhow, I know that some people are still disrespectful. How do you deal with all the hateful birds who criticize and spread false rumors? Good question. As a natural man, I sometimes get frustrated, but now I don't want to be a natural man anymore: I will strive to be supernatural because that is where true power dwells. Therefore, each time a disrespectful person approaches me, I use the opportunity to practice calmness and work on improving my smile.

I'm wondering why there's nothing about slavery in your black history book. Because slavery is not black history - slavery is the Caucasian history of colonialism.

How long have you been promoting black history, and what keeps you going? I have been teaching about black history for decades now, and have spoken to millions of people during that time. Many of these people are from all walks of life, and they lovingly support my efforts. They're my heat in the winter and my breeze in the summer - because they help to keep me going when the going gets tough. But ultimately speaking, it is the man upstairs who keeps me going.

The older edition of your black history book mentioned that God is a man. Is this true? Yes, it is. Exodus 15:3 (KJV) says that God is a man, and Habakkuk 3:3 says that God came from Teman (a place in Arabia), but He lives in Jerusalem (Psalms 9:11).

Holy shift! Do you really believe that God came from Arabia and that He is a man? It is in the scriptures - see for yourself.

I have noticed that you have a bonus section dedicated to health and wealth in your book. Why? Because health and wealth go perfectly together - they hug and kiss each other. To be financially rich but poor in health makes no sense at all. The man who is truly rich is a "good man" who is healthy, wealthy and wise.

I have known you to be a tough guy, even tougher than cornmeal dumplings. How do you keep your strength up while doing such massive work? For the guys who like to be hardy - beef helps to keep your strength up. It is the meat of choice for athletes and fighters. Nevertheless, it is best to eat lots of fruits and vegetables. Fruits and vegetables give life, while beef produces strength.

Then why do some guys eat steak for dinner, while some men eat nothing but dirt? For real, I know a few guys who eat nothing but dry dirt. It all boils down to money. Because money is at the root of every problem, especially in a capitalistic society.

What about the sophisticated person who can afford good food - what would you recommend for dinner? I would recommend sardines for dinner (smile). But snapper fish with lots of organic fruits and vegetables should be good. And remember, fish is one of the most nutrient-dense food on the planet, and sardines are the most nutritious of all fish.

Wow, that was some shocking knowledge. You've been a true champion. Thank you for your time and profound insight. Do you have any final words for the reader? Well, sure. I would say - live your life and pick your "good dreams" up off the ground, then work cheerfully to turn them into reality… and remember to flow gracefully around obstacles like water - it is one of the most flexible substances in the universe.

This is a special collector's item

Certified to be 100% awesome by King Majesty

Ways to care for your black history book

- Avoid folding or crushing
- Avoid getting dog-ears onto the edges
- Keep in a clean place and avoid mud
- Keep in a safe place to avoid theft

In the event that your black history book is damaged, lost or stolen; then pay King Majesty a visit, he would be more than happy to sell you another one.

PART 2

BONUS SECTION

"Gold is the money of kings, silver is the money of gentlemen, barter is the money of peasants - but debt is the money of slaves." – Norm Franz

"I counsel you to buy from me gold, that you may be rich" – Jesus (Revelations 3:18, NKJV)

The 10 Financial Commandments

NOTE: THIS IS NOT FINANCIAL ADVICE. THESE ARE THE AUTHOR'S COMMANDMENTS THAT HE USED TO ACCUMULATE WEALTH.

1. Thou shall save and accumulate real money - gold and silver and avoid saving trash. Remember, cash is trash because it has no intrinsic value. Meanwhile, gold and silver have been used as real money and cherished since ancient antiquity. Gold is from a supernova star that exploded many years ago, while cash is just pieces of paper with pictures of dead guys printed on them. The United States Constitution clearly states that only gold and silver can be legal tender, and it forbids paper money or bills of credit.

2. Thou must equip thyself with the requisite knowledge about money. The-powers-that-be make sure that they don't teach anything about money in school - so that all these old boys and girls will eventually grow up and become slaves for the rich - this is accomplished by keeping the people ignorant about money and keeping them trapped in perpetual labor, like a hamster on a wheel.

3. Thou shall avoid holding idle cash. Whenever I get a piece of paper with a dead guy printed on it, I quickly exchange it for real money or use it to purchase amazing assets like Litecoin and other cryptocurrencies (a revolutionary technology and the hottest investment in the universe). Why would a person with knowledge ever want to save paper money when it loses 3-5% of its value each year through inflation? Remember, the U.S. dollar has lost more than 99% of its value since 1913.

4. Thou must not follow in the ways of the poor. Poor people are spenders, while rich people are investors. It is shocking to see that virtually all rich folks are owners of stocks, land, real estate, and other forms of investments, while it is quite disturbing to see poor people spending all their money with no desire to invest.

5. Thou shall not get into debt. The word debt is closely related to the word death. The powers that be are trying to force-feed the masses a "manure sandwich" - by telling the people to use debt. But luckily, this book was designed to guide the reader - so that the reader will not step on a banana peel.

6. Thou shall learn how to enjoy thy wealth in the proper way - have fun and live life the way that you desire, spending no more than 50% of your income each year.

7. Thou shall know the truth about money - all it takes to acquire wealth is to be good with your money and change your mindset from being a spender to an investor.

8. Thou shall control thy expenditures and avoid wasting thy money on trivial things - this is the key area that needs your attention. Remember, it is not difficult to acquire money - the greatest challenge is to keep it.

9. Thou must consistently and persistently allocate a portion of thy income towards investments. Some people allocate 10%, while I strive to set aside 90%. Land provides food and shelter, and it's easy to eliminate expenses when you own land. The UN and EU are pushing hard for the masses to start eating insects, and if the so-called elites have it their way, the masses will eat bugs while they eat steak, fish, fruits, and vegetables. Singapore recently approved 16 different types of insects available for purchase in supermarkets and restaurants for human consumption, while in some countries, people are starting to eat ants. But I say all that to say this - if you don't want to be a part of their creepy plans, own land and grow your own food.

10. Be good with thy money. It is the ultimate secret to acquire wealth.

Note: never be the aggressor in words or actions. Keep the peace!

"How far you go in life depends on your being tender with the young, compassionate with the aged, sympathetic with the striving and tolerant of the weak and strong. Because someday in your life you will have been all of these." – George Washington Carver

Romance Without Finance

— romance without finance is a nuisance —

I'm sure you have probably heard the expression; romance without finance is a nuisance. Well, the funny thing about it is - it is true. A whopping 95% of problems in relationships are of a financial nature. If you care deeply about love and relationships, then it is imperative for you to be good with your money. Most women instinctively know, and they wonder why so many men are so broke. They know that money is important and men should have it in abundance, but when they look around and see so many broke guys, they often wonder among themselves.

In traditional Eastern cultures and older civilizations, the first thing for a man to do is to acquire wealth. In ancient times, a man had to have wealth before he could marry the neighbor's daughter. That was the way of our forefathers, and it is the way of the wise and prudent. Some couples can overcome the relationship hurdles without finance, but this is exceedingly rare.

Very few relationships are successful without finance — some merely survive, which is not what you want. You don't just want your relationship to survive - emphatically, no! You want your relationship to flourish to its fullest potential. In order to do that, you must be good with your money and acquire wealth.

Love recognizes no barriers. It jumps hurdles, leaps fences, penetrates walls to arrive at its destination full of hope. - Maya Angelou

Money Talent

"Money answers all things" - Ecclesiastes 10:19

There is a parable that speaks of money in a very profound and unique way. I will attempt to tell it clearly and concisely - so that the reader may glimpse how important it is to be good with money.

There was a king who had to go away for some time to a faraway land. The king had three servants - one, he gave five talents (money) - the next, he gave two talents - and the other, he gave one talent. He then told the servants that if they are good with the money, on his return, he would reward them. He then departed.

The man with five talents was exceptionally good with his money, and in turn, he doubled it to ten. The man with two talents was also good with his money, and he doubled it to four talents. But the man with one talent was quite wasteful and did not appreciate the small - but precious money he had. He buried his one talent and was upset at the master for giving him only one.

On the king's return, he was incredibly pleased with the servant who increased his five talents to ten. He told him, "Well done, thou good and faithful servant, **because you've been faithful over little - I will make you ruler over much, enter thou into thy joy."**

The man who had two talents presented four talents to the king. The king said, "Well done, thou good and faithful servant, because you've been faithful over little - I will make you ruler over much, enter thou into thy joy."

The servant who buried his one talent presented no increase and started to accuse the master. Surprisingly, the servant who didn't do anything to grow or increase the talent was the one with the most disrespect. The master told him that he was a wicked and slothful servant - and told the others to take the talent from the slothful servant and give it to the man that has ten - for to him who has, more shall be given, but to him who has not, even that shall be taken away.

Bottom line: if we appreciate money, then we would have it. Not having money is proof enough to show that we don't cherish it.

New Dark Age

The "Dark Age" was a time that signified the decline of the European empire, marked by war, famine, and plague. **Meanwhile, Africa was on the rise, so much so that the richest man in the world was an African (Mansa Musa).** The "New Dark Age" will be similar to the "Dark Age". Our African brothers and sisters and people of African descent will attain great wealth and prosperity.

NOTE: Africa is the richest continent, with 65% of the world's uncultivated arable land. However, if you live in North America, Europe, or Asia, you might want to: **1. Double-time and get your financial house in order** 2. Stockpile non-perishable food items **3. WATCH THE WEATHER** 4. Make sure you're in **THE RIGHT PLACE.**

Friendly Reminders

1. Let us remind ourselves that the blacks and natives in North America are in the same boat together, **and we should have nothing but love for our native brothers and sisters.** They're some of the kindest people I've ever met.

2. While you're on the journey to financial riches, remember to practice empathy. After meeting millions of people, I can tell you with confidence that the kindest and most compassionate people are the ones who are dirt-poor. Many financially rich people have very little empathy. Therefore, the richer you become, the more empathy you can strive to attain.

3. Eat lots of fruits and vegetables, drink clean and pure spring water, get lots of sunshine, fresh air, and exercise. And Remember to consume red onions instead of the white ones. Red onions contain lots of natural medicine (quercetin). And stay away from the devil's food (pork and insects).

4. Whatever life throws at you, remember that you're the best. You can surmount any obstacle because where there's a will, there's a way.

5. If you encounter a difficult task, break it down into small sections to make it easy. Good luck on your journey.

"When you learn, teach. When you get, give." — Maya Angelou

Don't sit down and wait for the opportunities to come. Get up and make them. — Madam C. J. Walker (the first female self-made millionaire in the history of America).

I have learned over the years that when one's mind is made up, this diminishes fear. — Rosa Parks

If you look at what you have in life, you'll always have more. If you look at what you don't have in life, you'll never have enough. — Oprah Winfrey

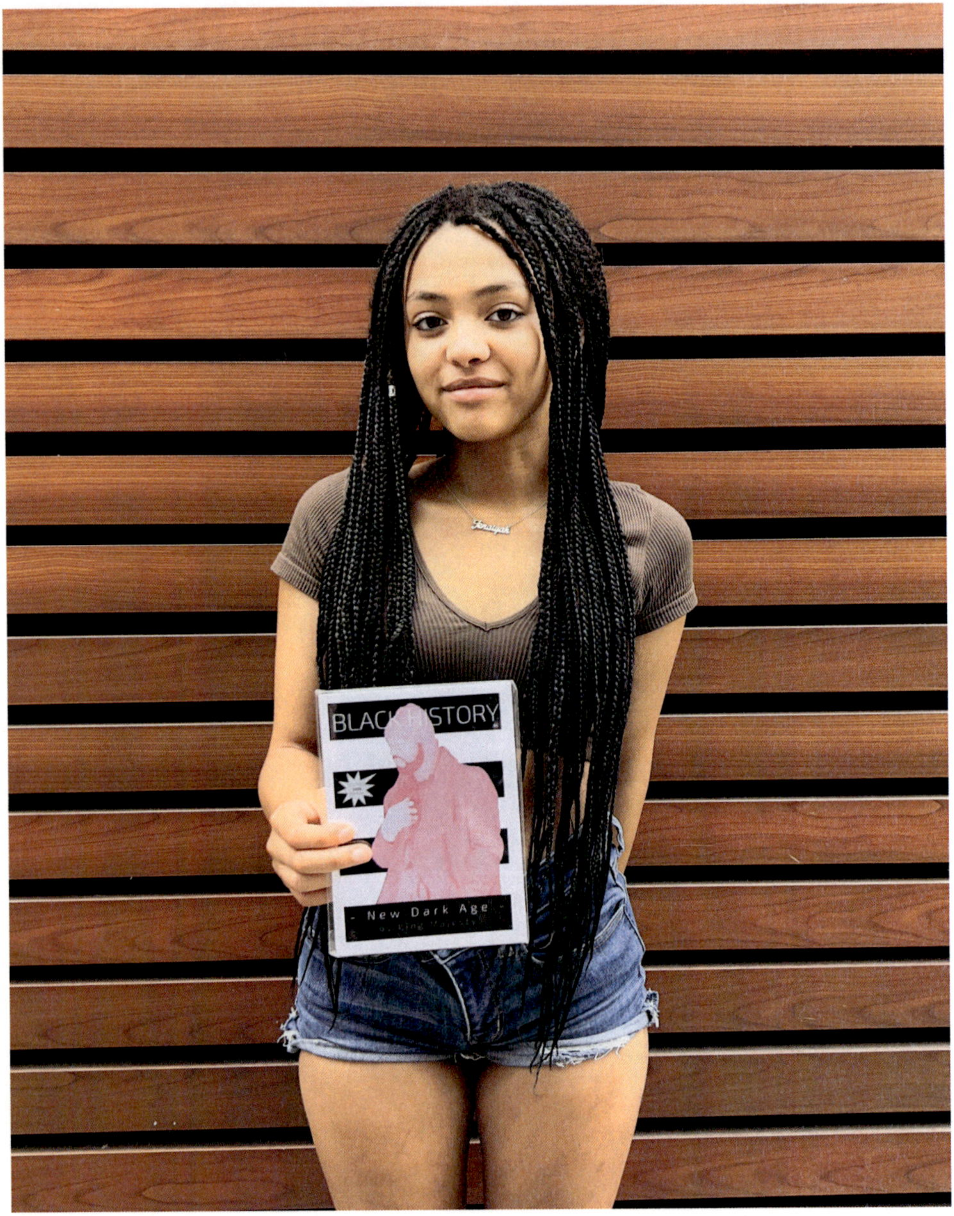

Knowledge speaks, but wisdom listens. — Jimmy Hendrix (the greatest guitarist in history).

He who is blessed is not disturbed.
— African proverb (Kenyan quote from Kanga and Swahili).

"It isn't where you come from; it's where you're going that counts." — Ella Fitzgerald (The Queen of Jazz).

"Hate is too great a burden to bear. It injures the hater more than it injures the hated." —
Coretta Scott King

He who is not courageous enough to take risks will accomplish nothing in life. — Muhammad Ali

Truth is powerful and it prevails. — Sojourner Truth

Do some pantry stacking. Stack up on dry beans, sardines, rice, flour, salt, spices, dried herbs, and whatever you can get your hands on. Those who are well-prepared wouldn't have to eat ants or other insects to survive . - King Majesty

"And he shall be like a tree planted in the streets of Toronto."

If you want to lift yourself up, lift up someone else. — Booker T. Washington

Live Your Life

and live it well

9781775394747
20250524004422

Made in Canada by LoginPOD
Powered by Publishers' Graphics
loginpod.ca

PGCA2024